ANTI-STRESS COLORING BOOK

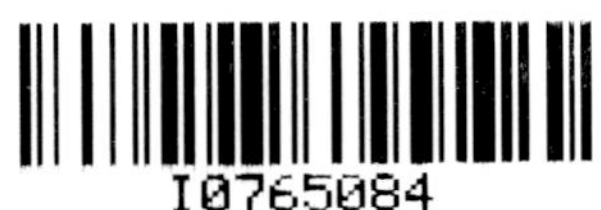

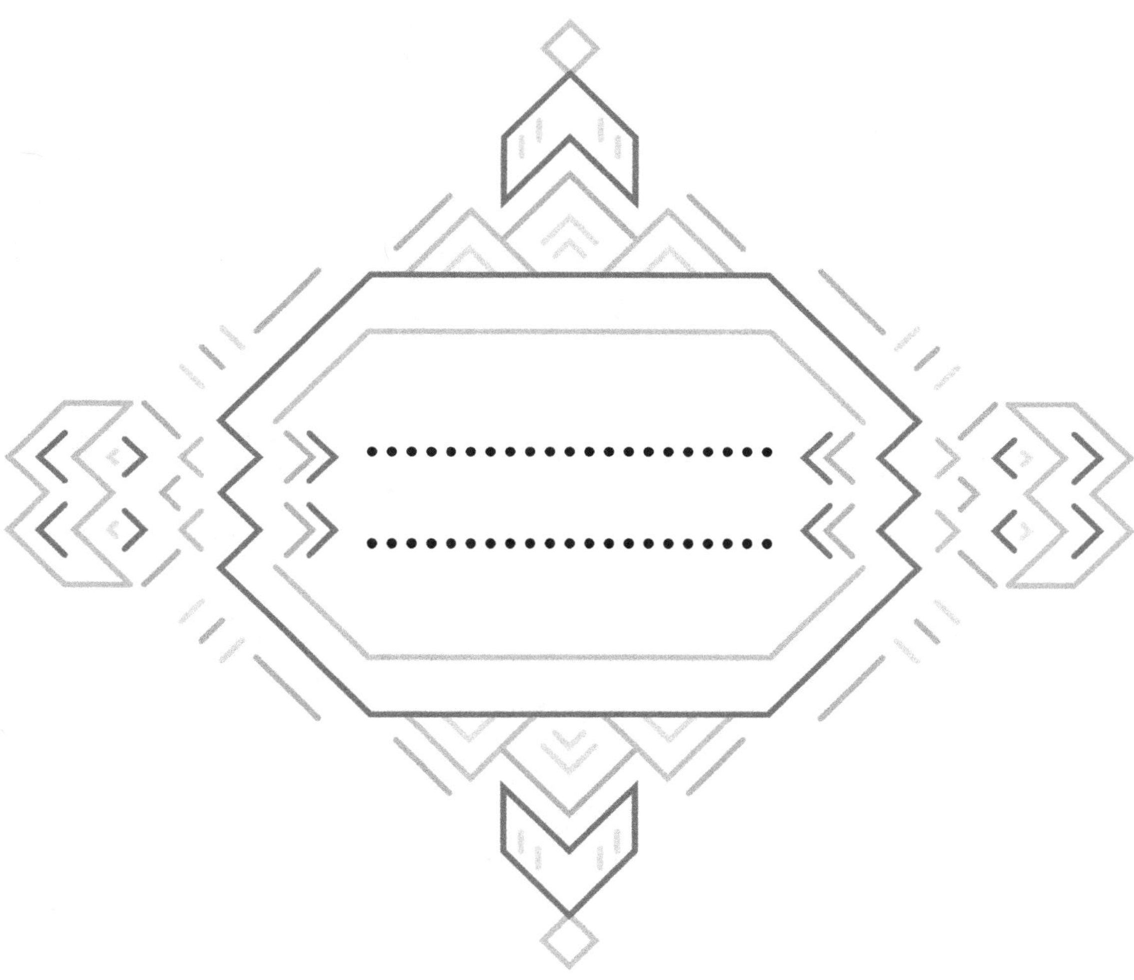

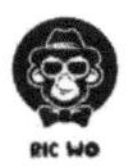

VOL 8

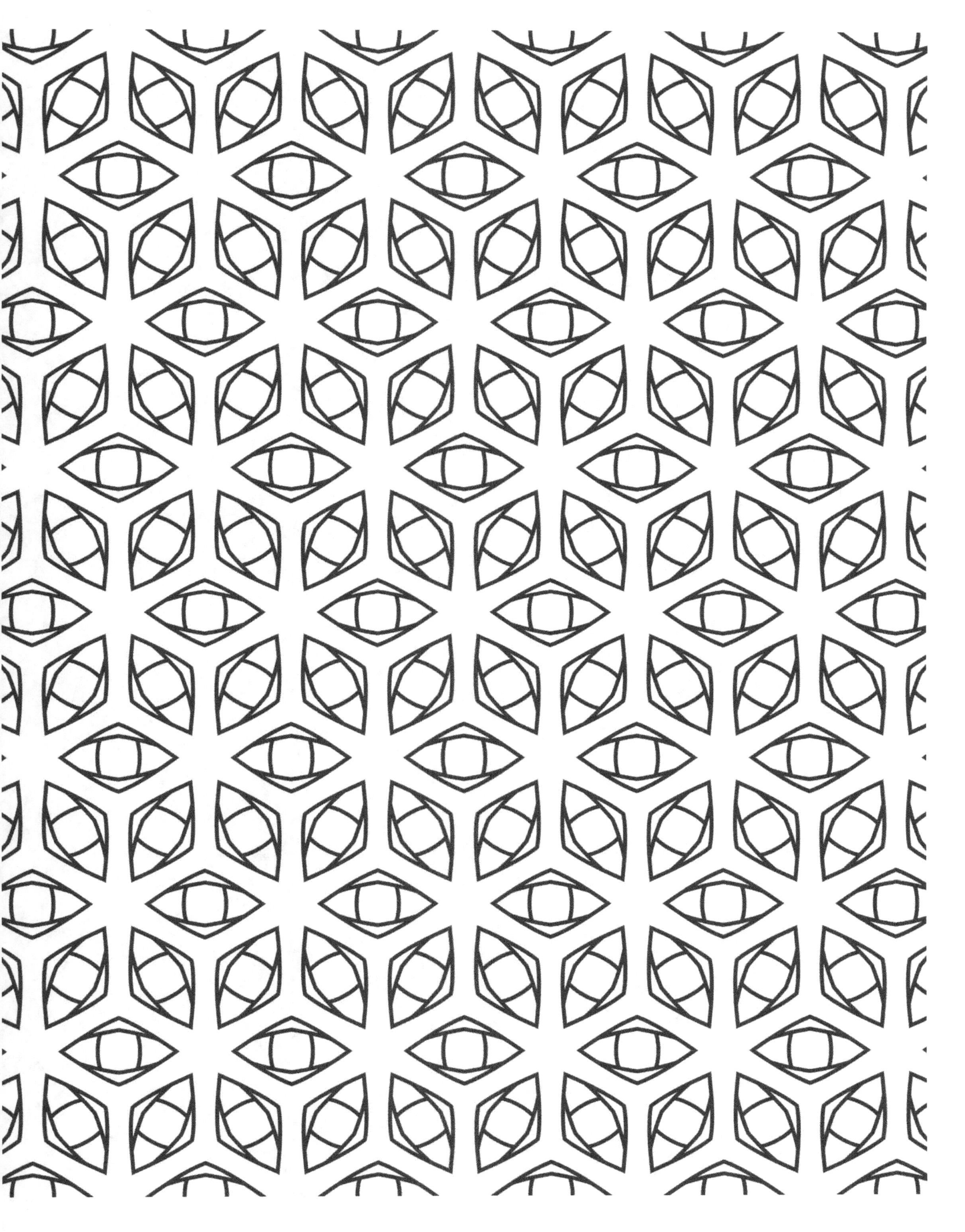

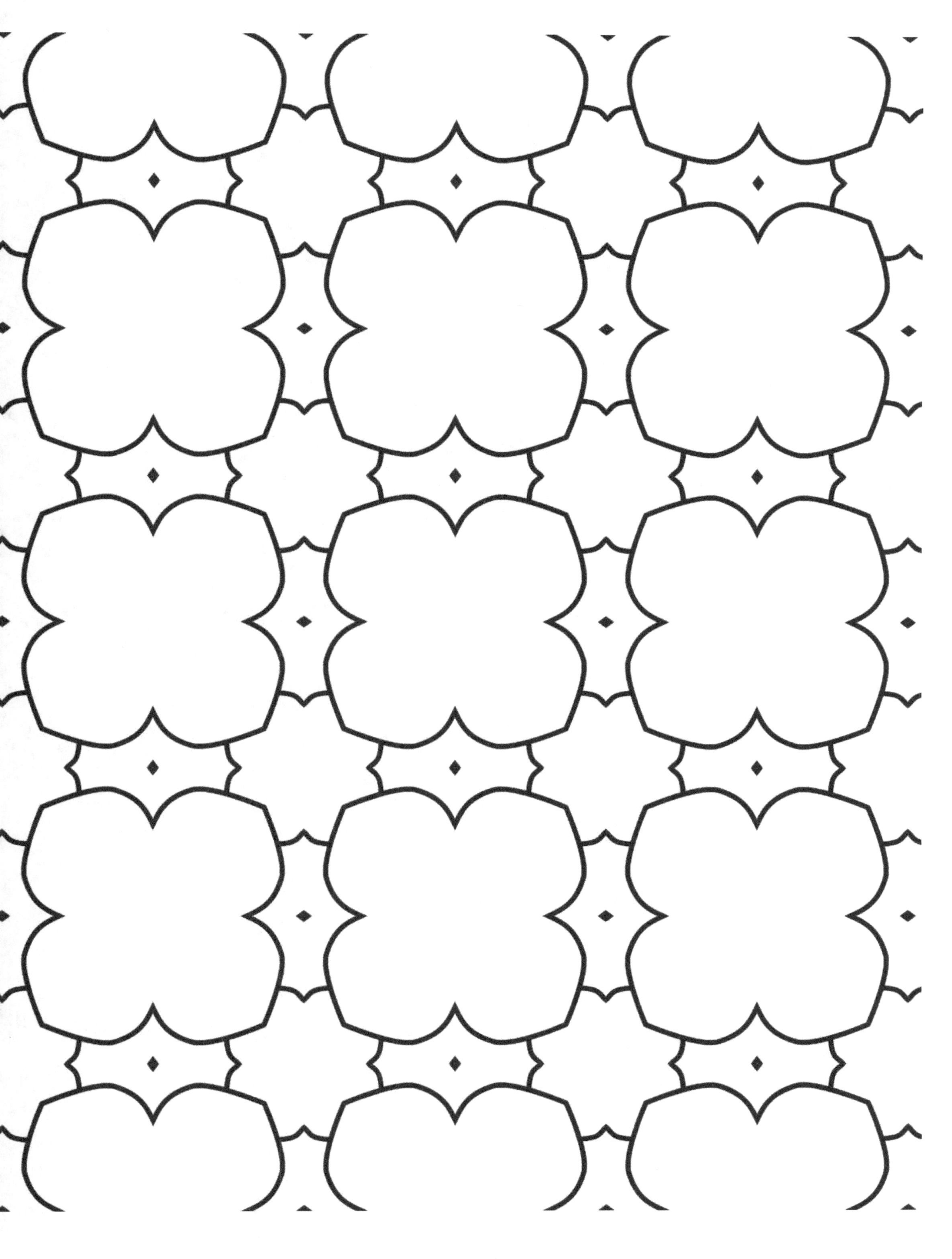

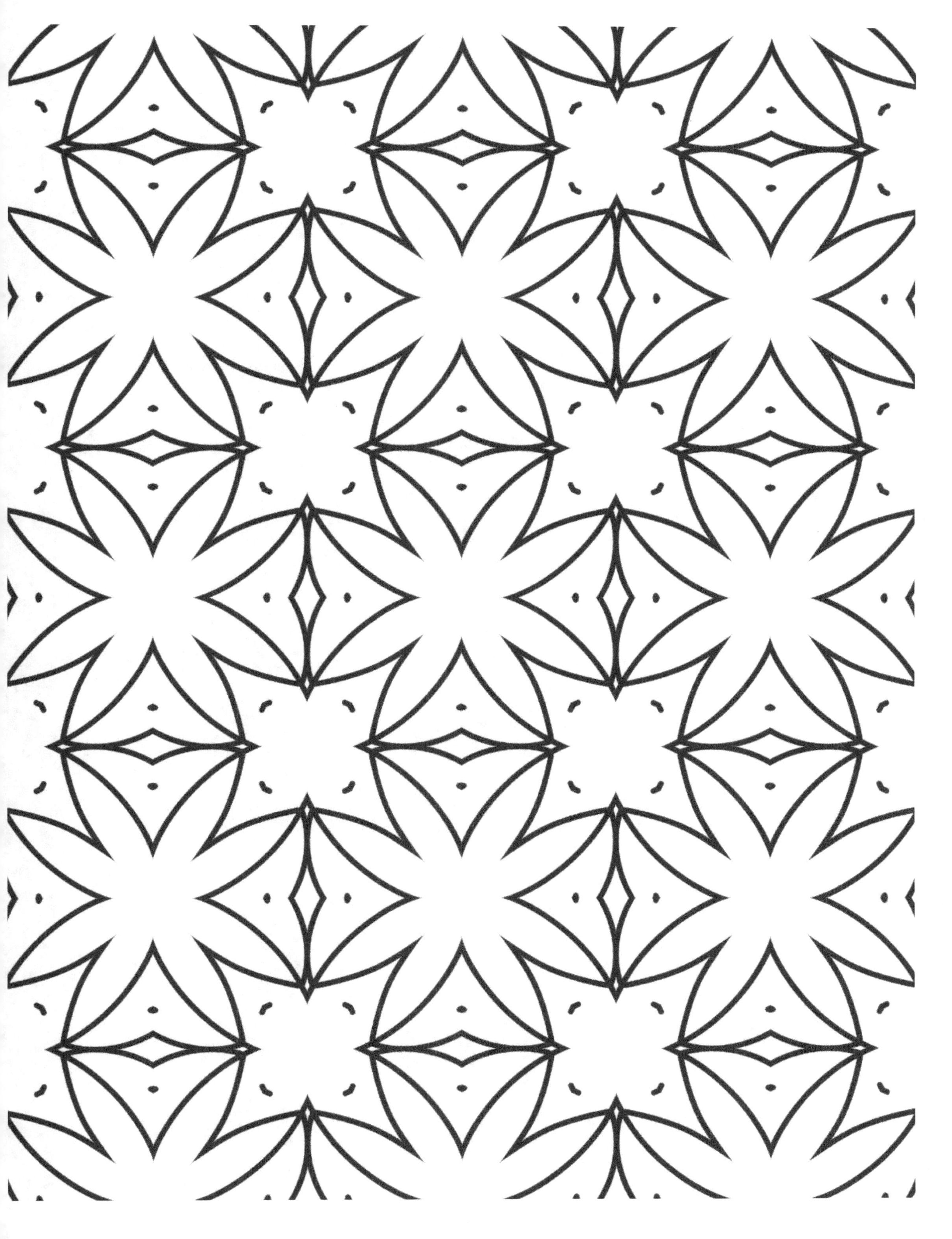

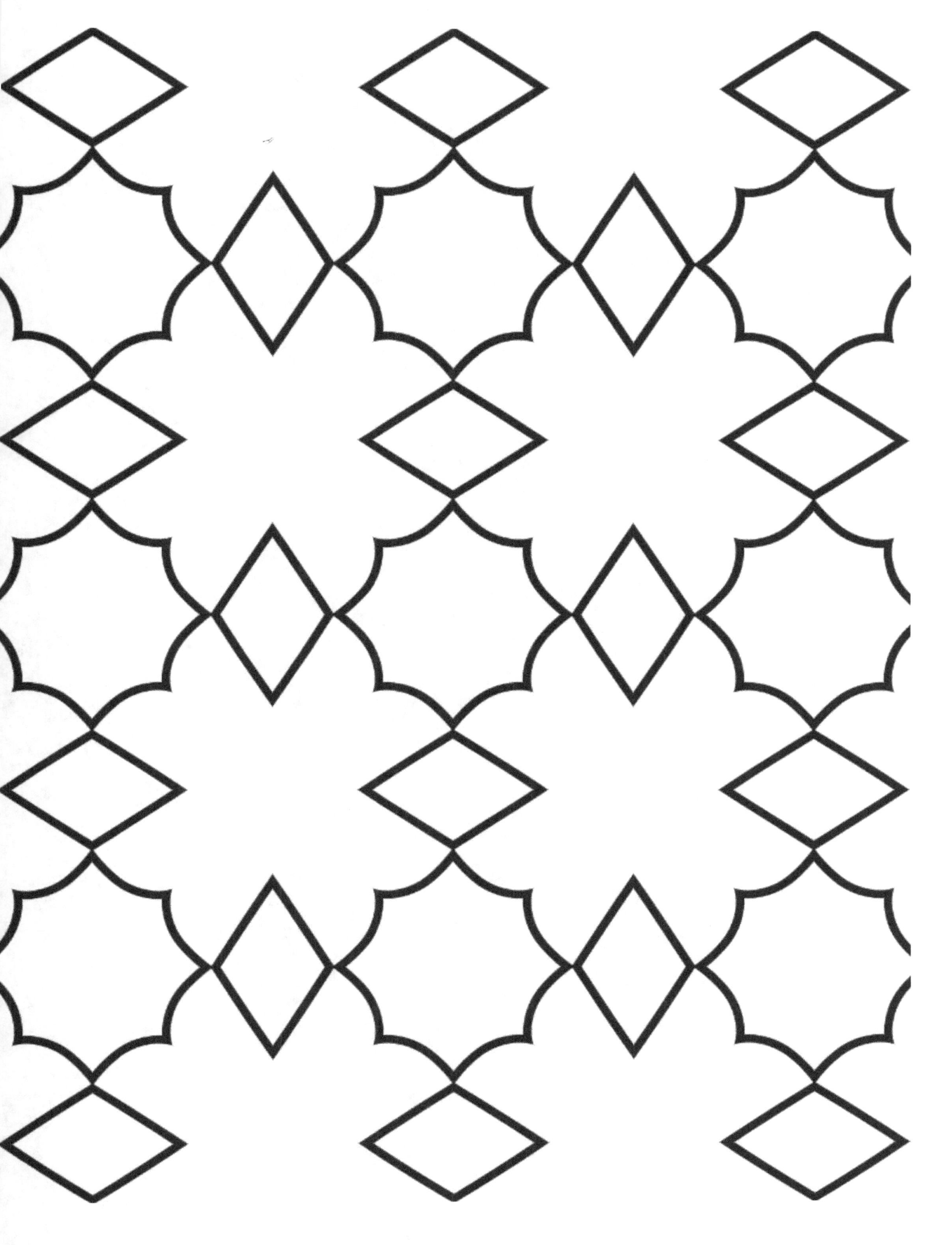

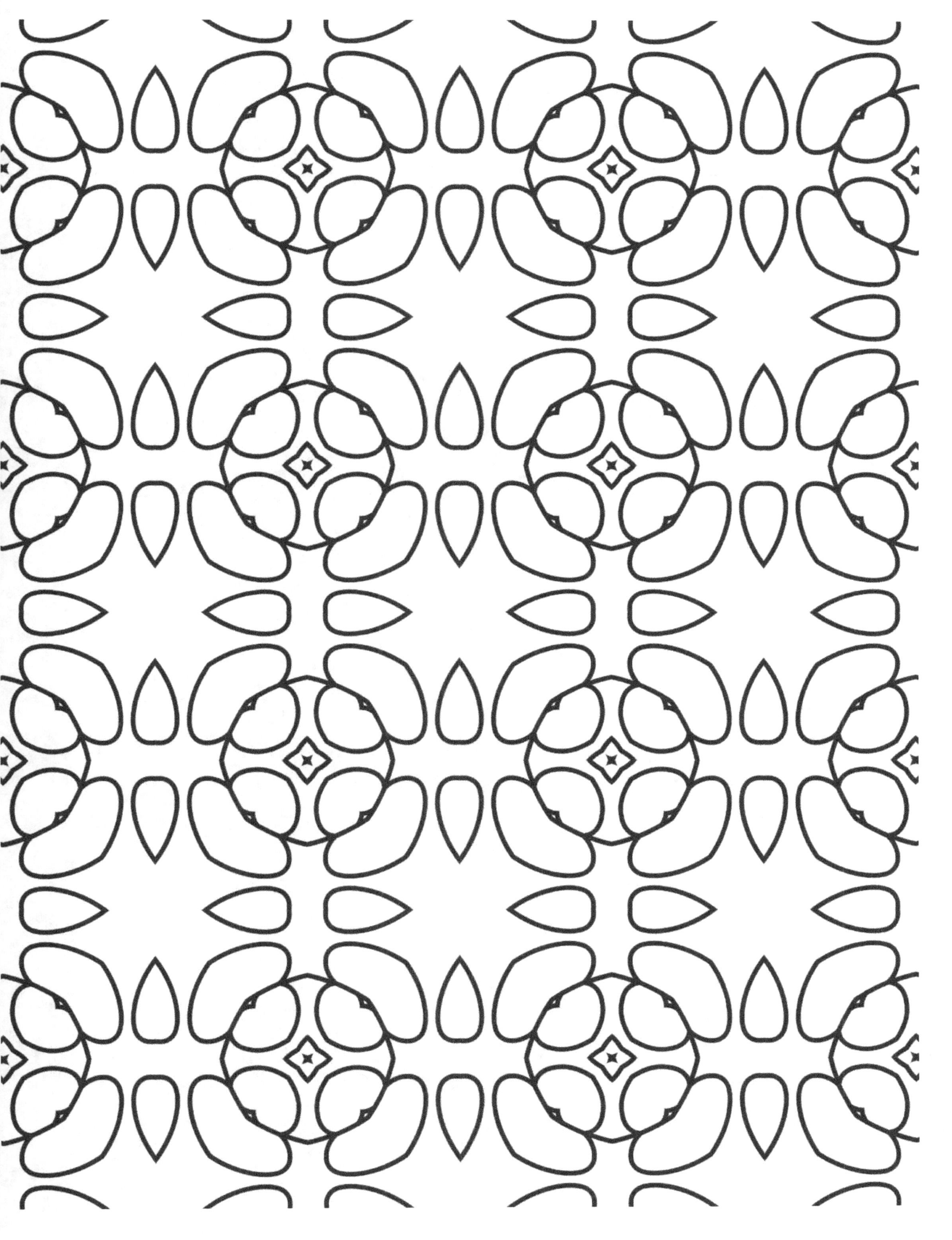

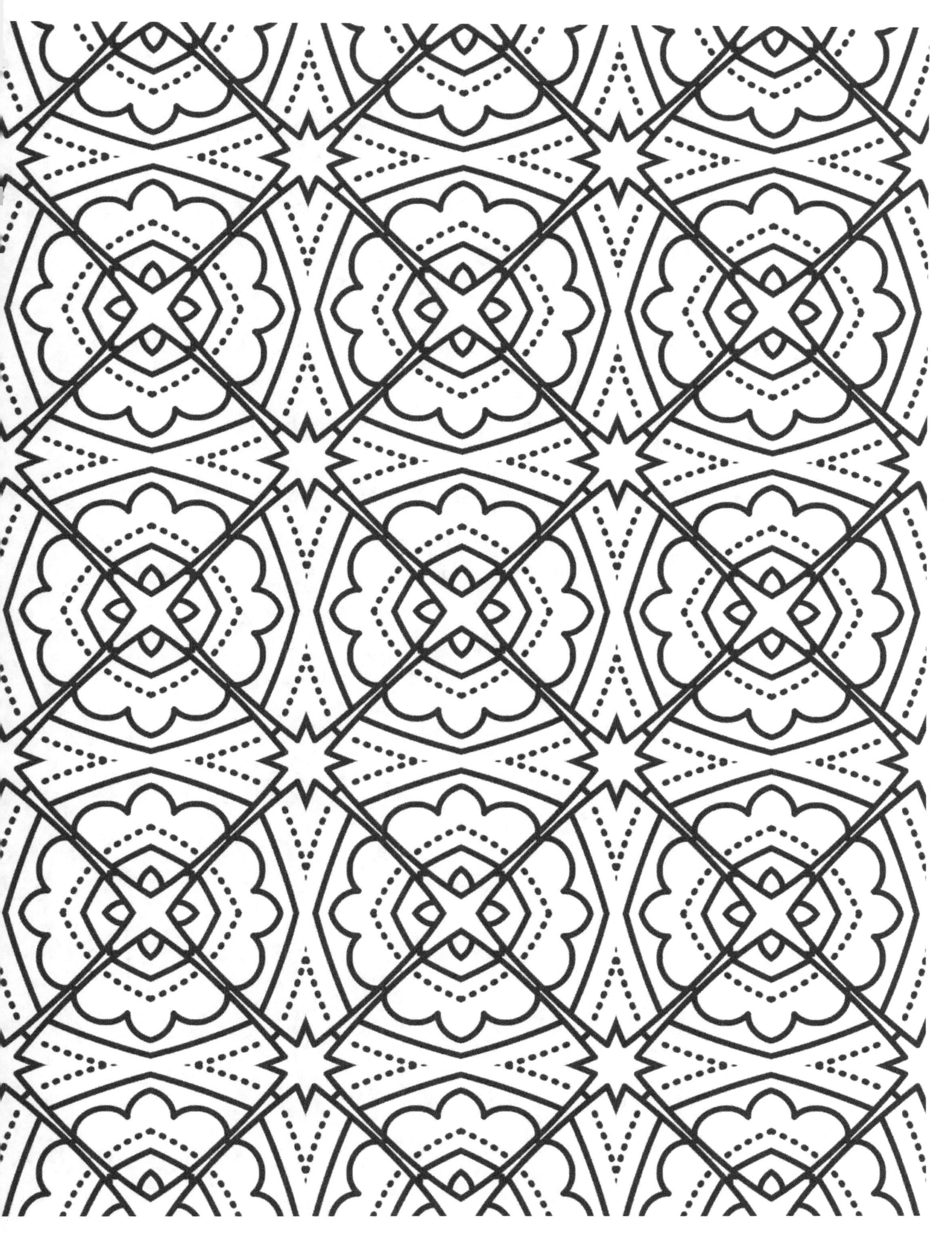

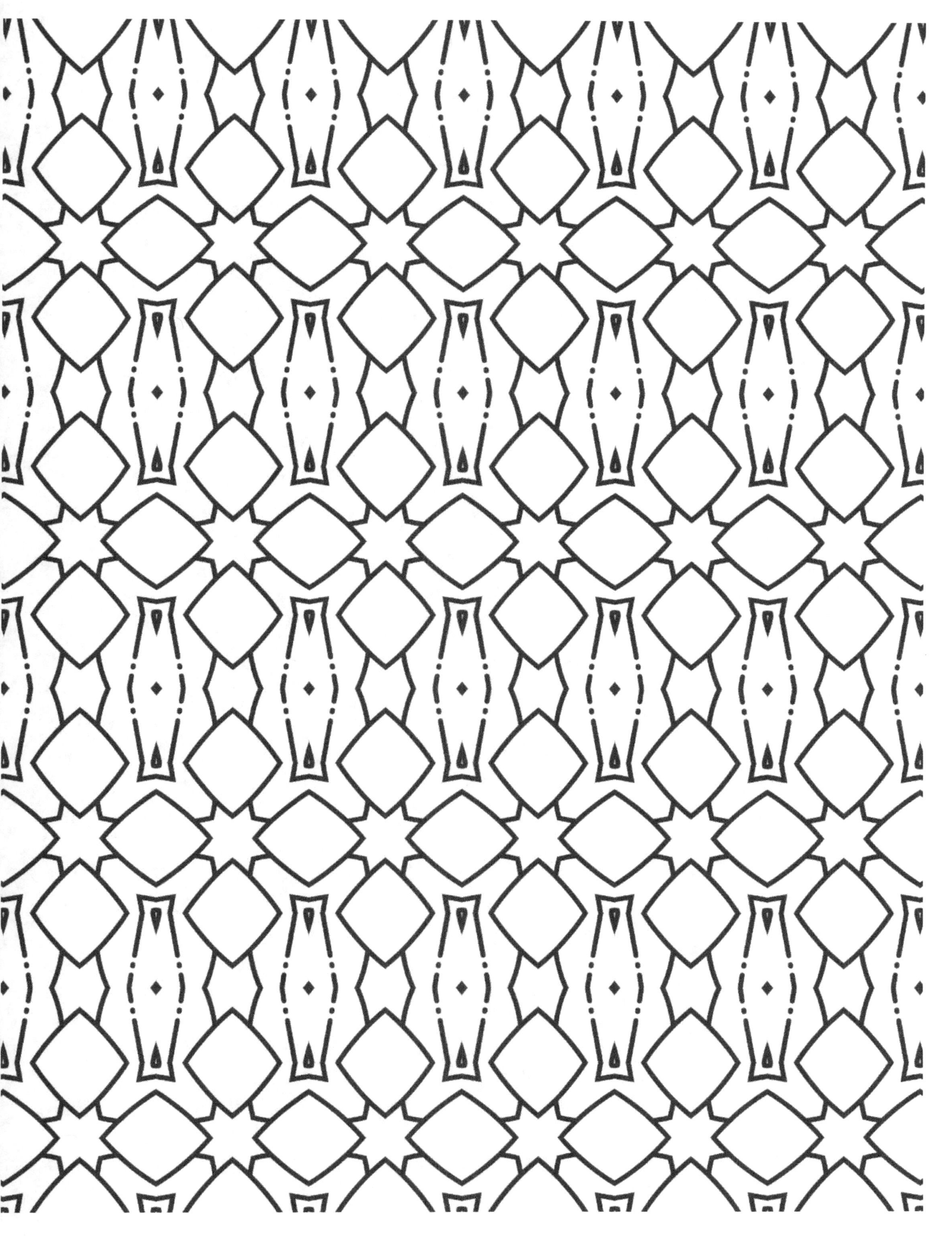

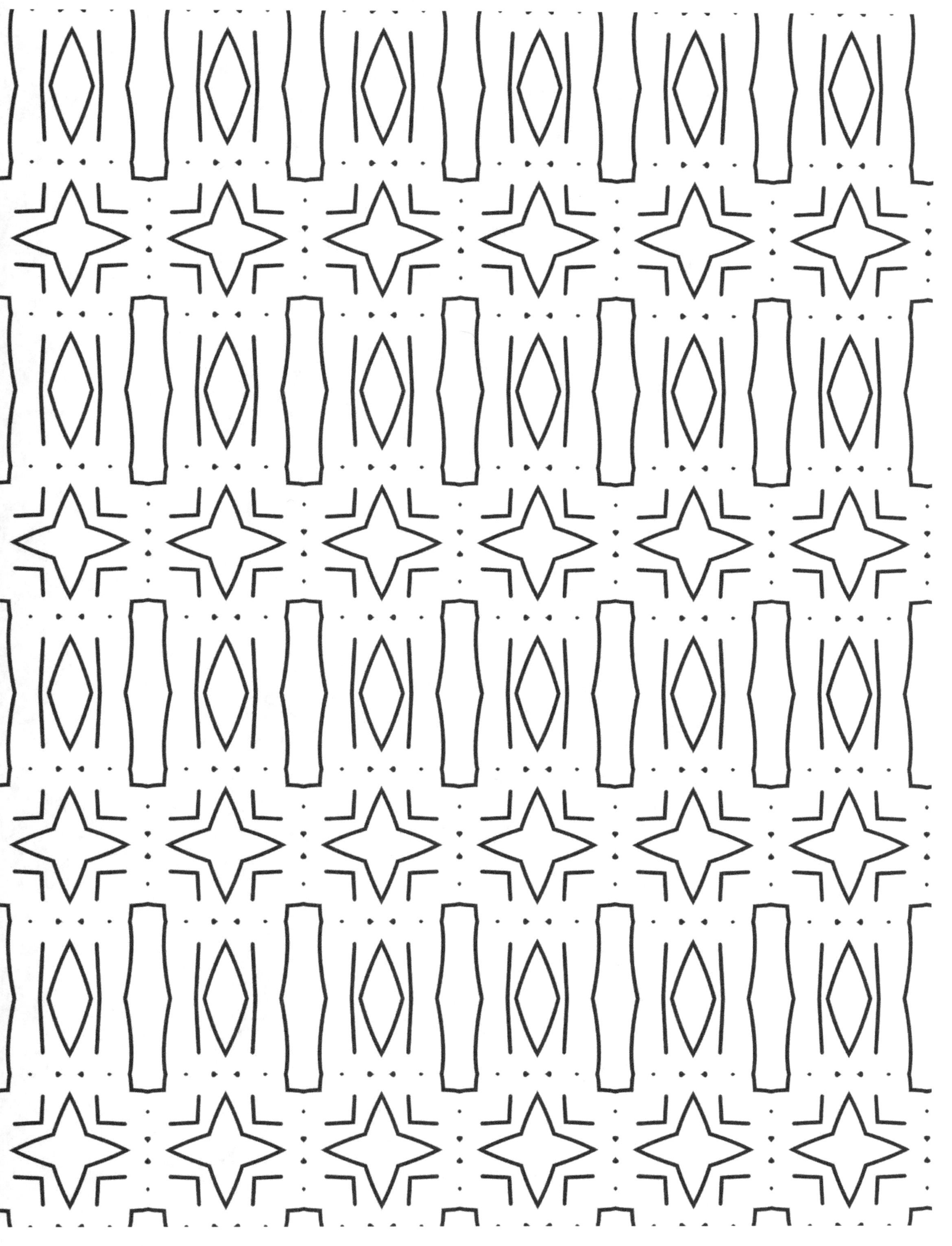

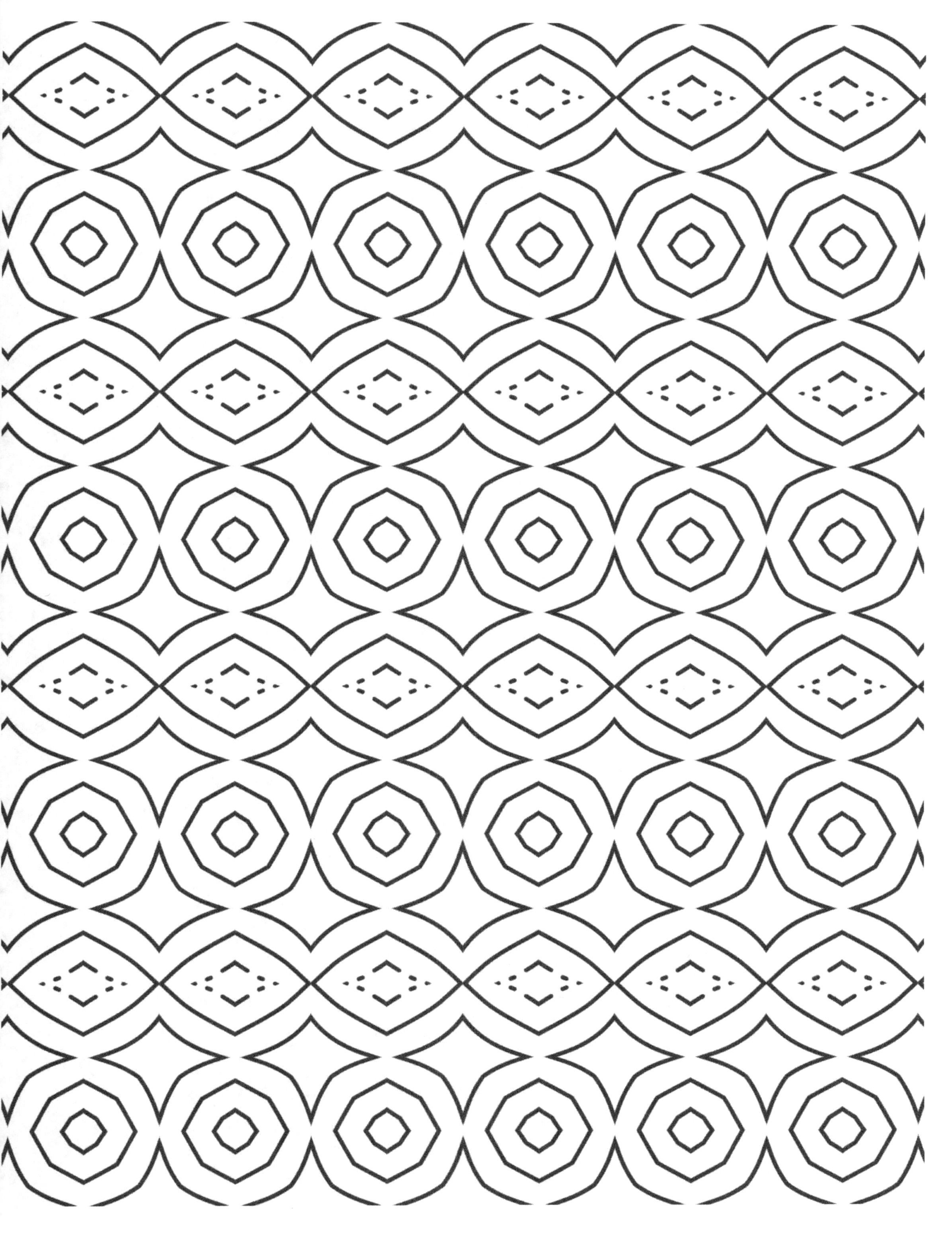

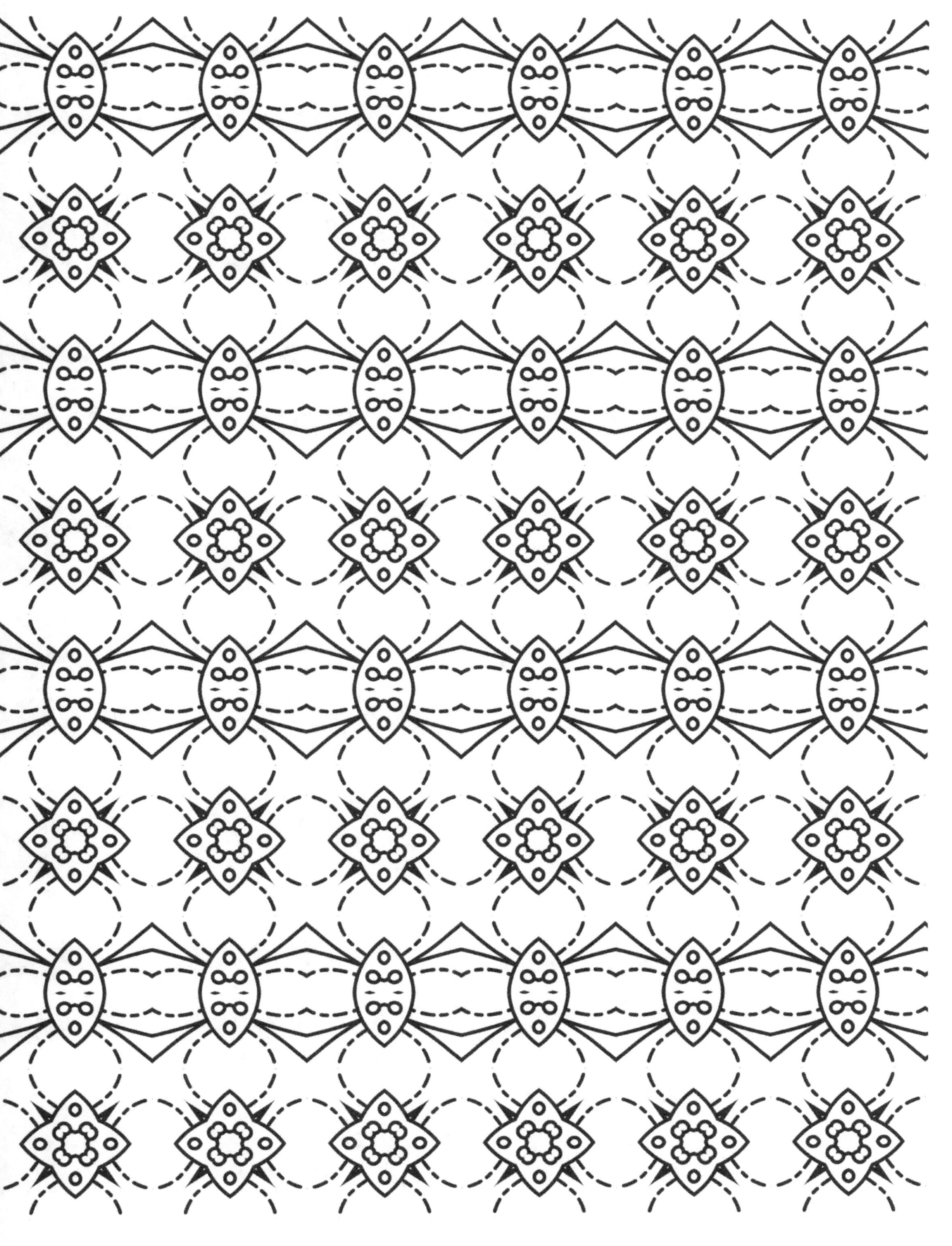

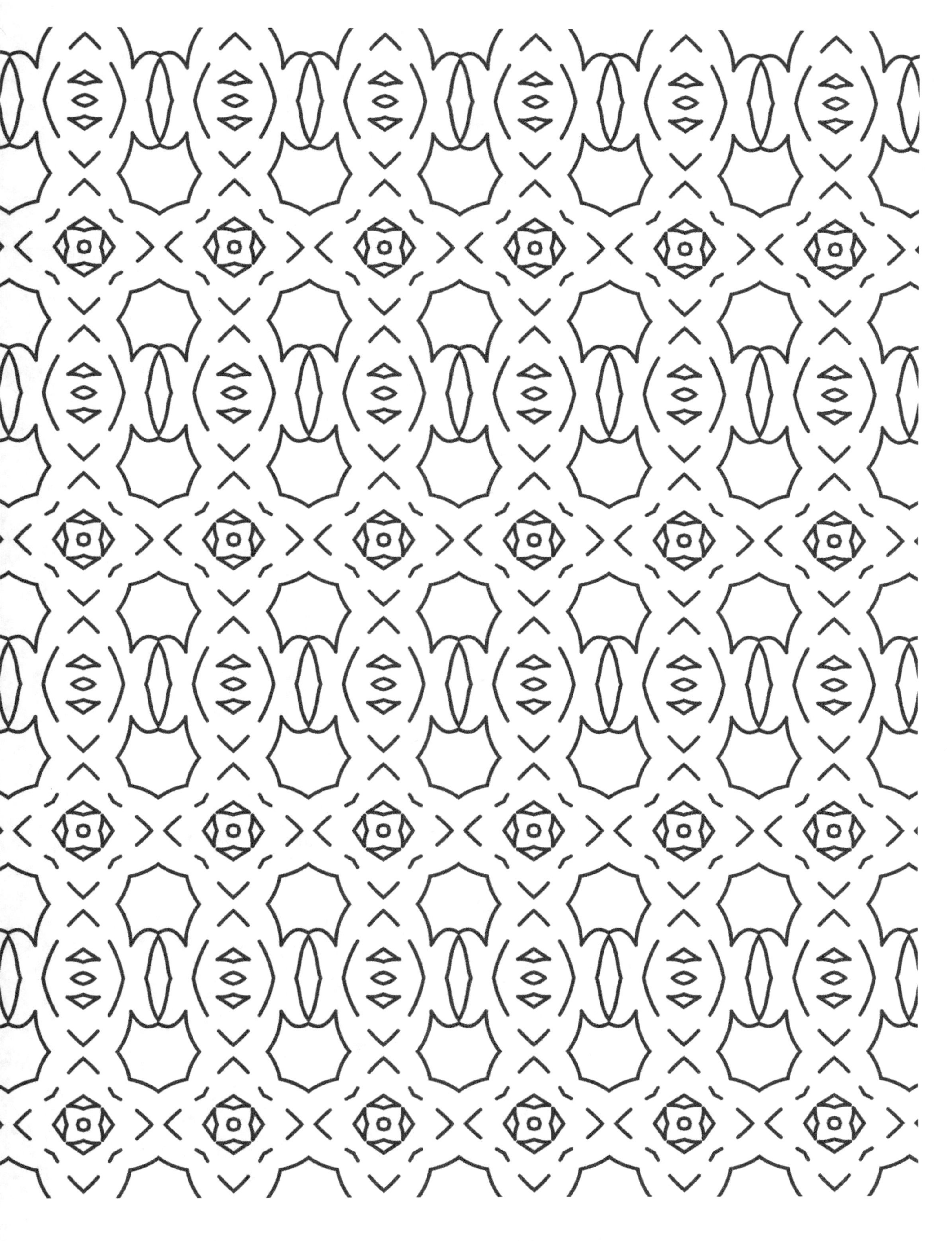

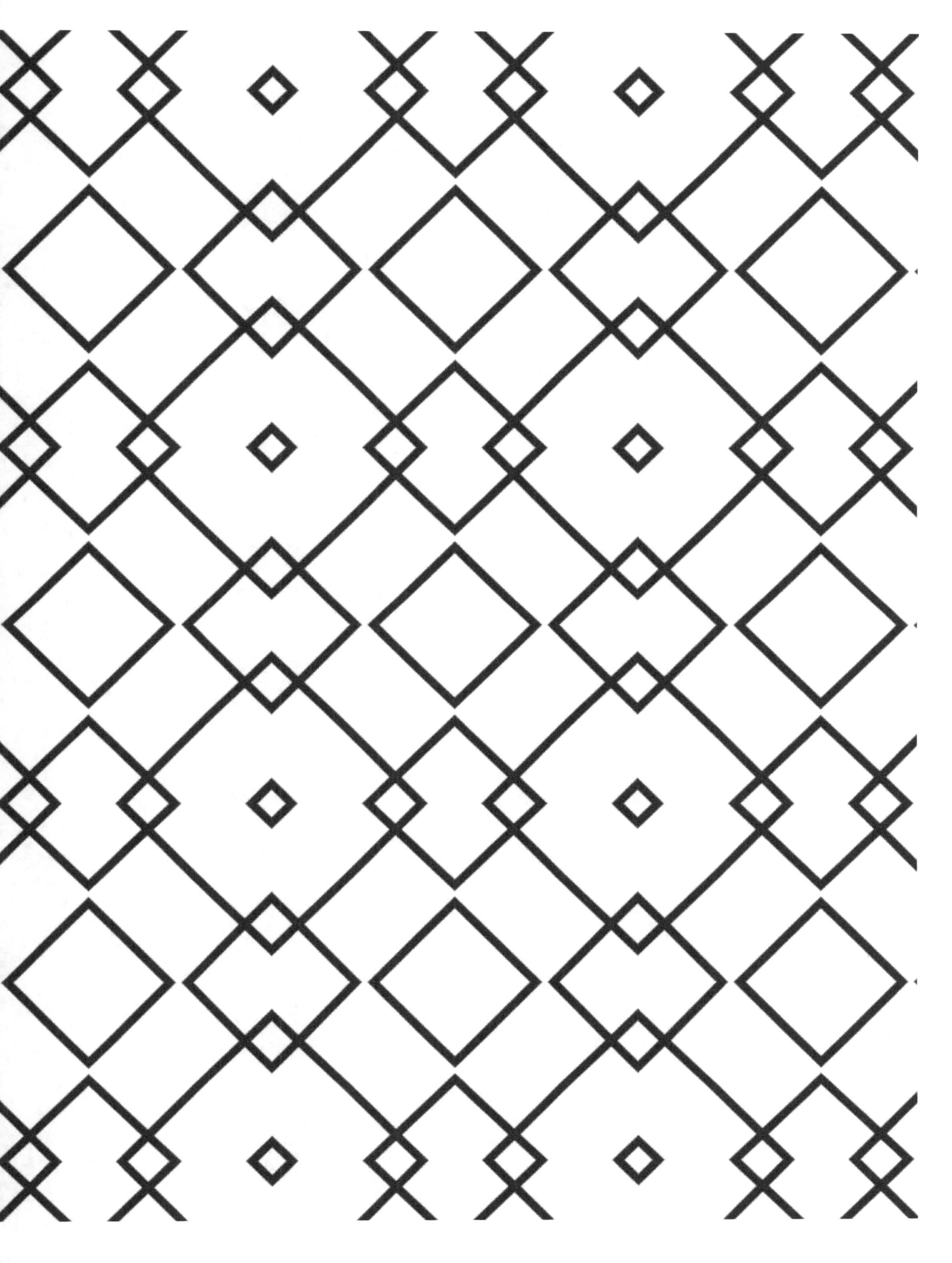

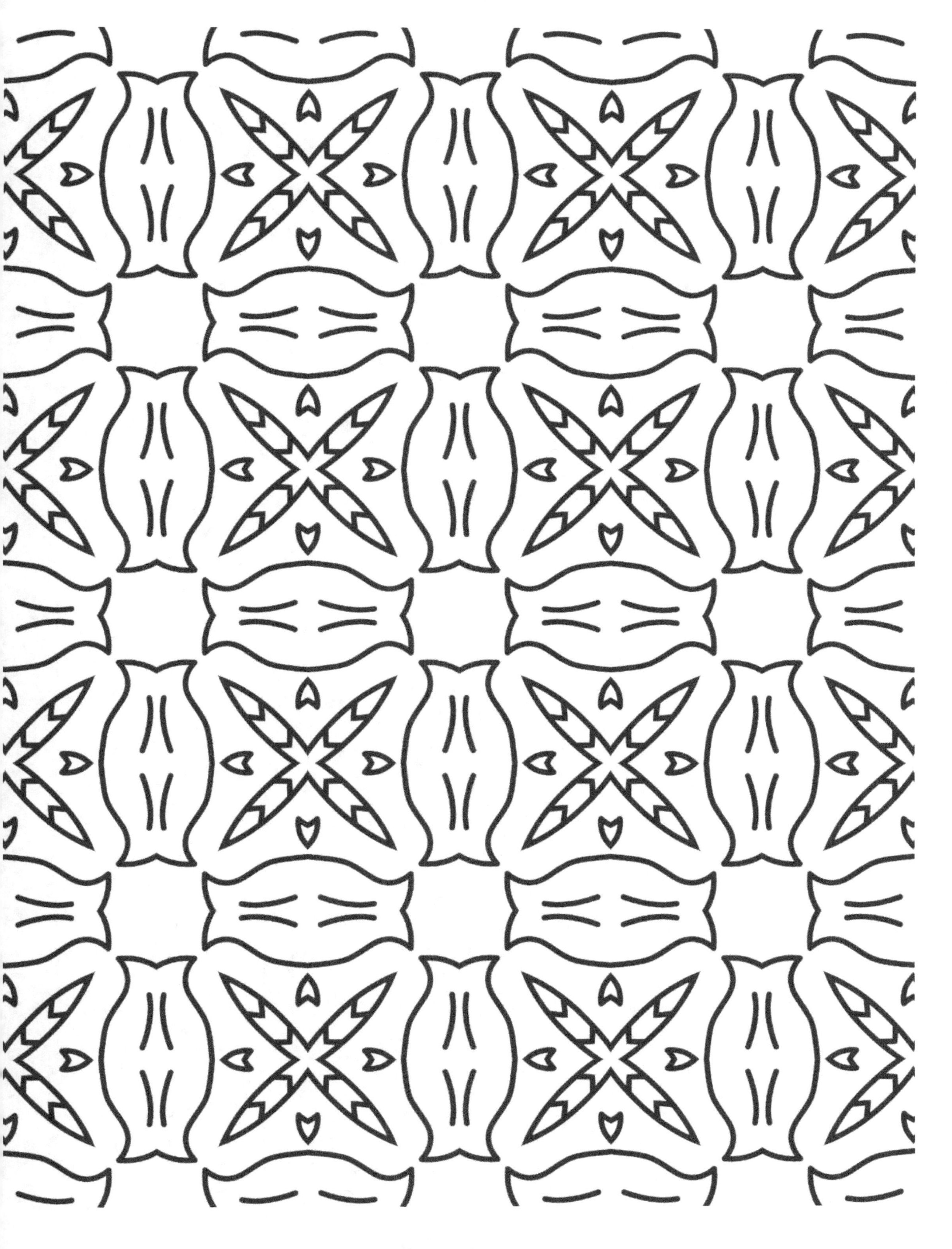

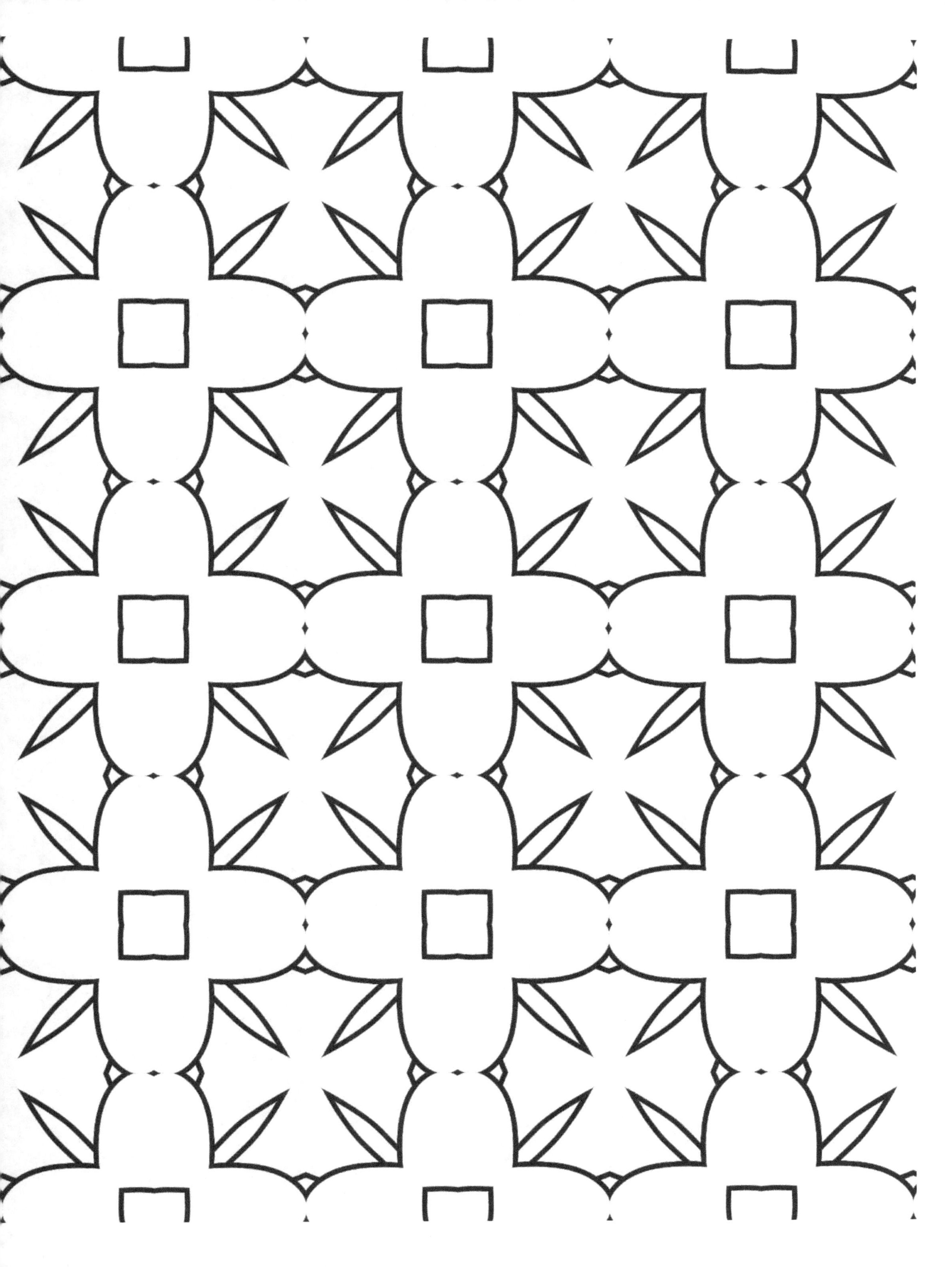

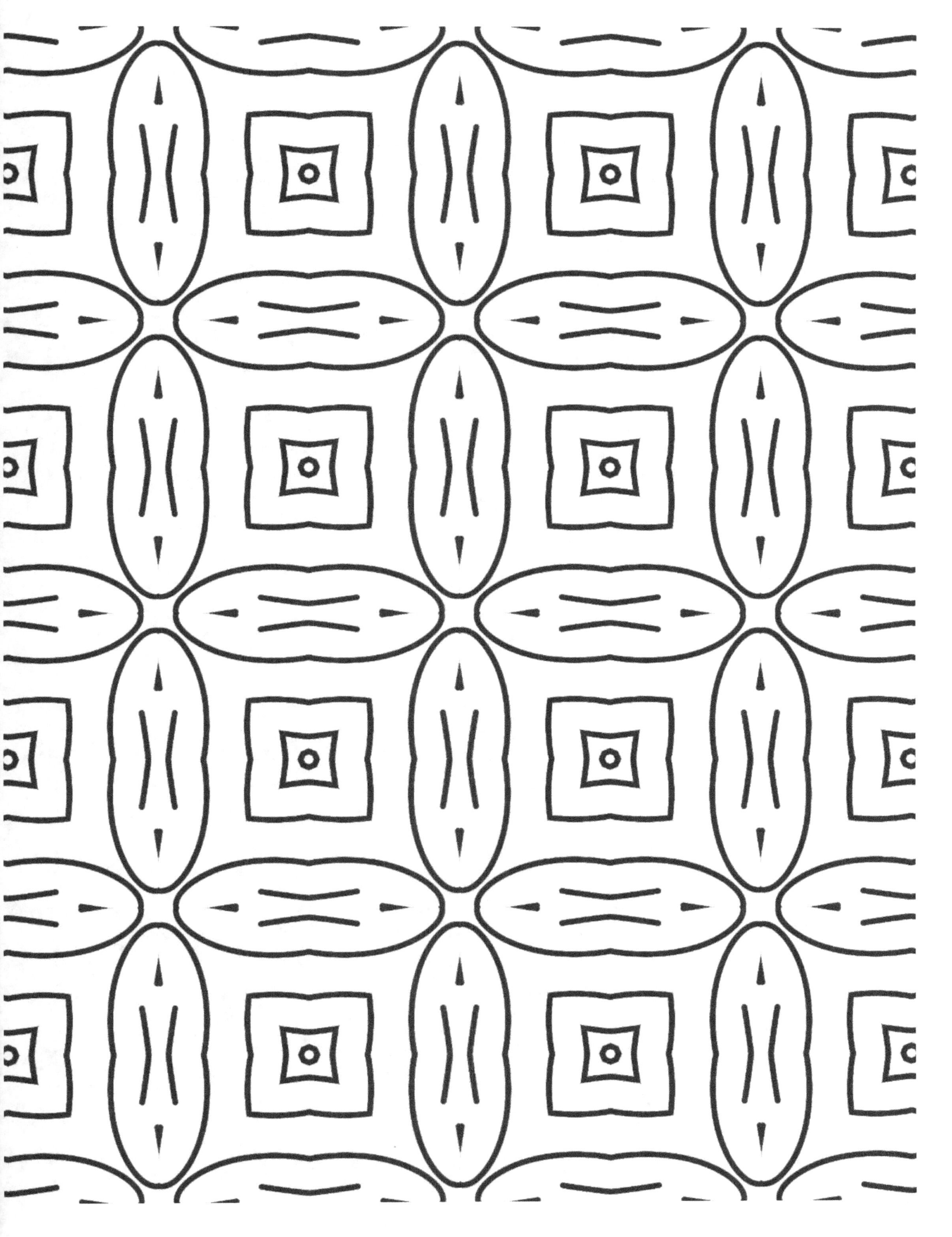

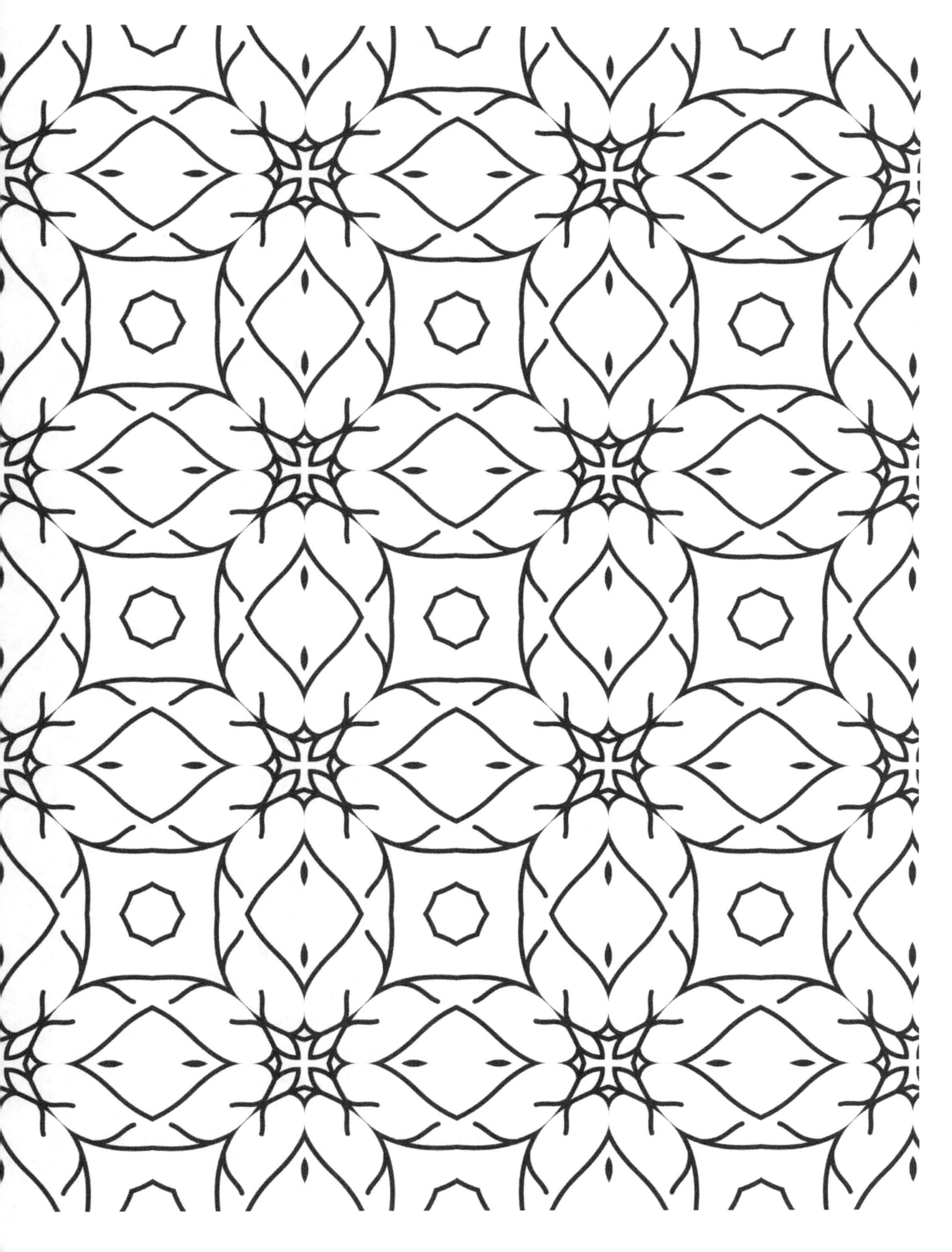

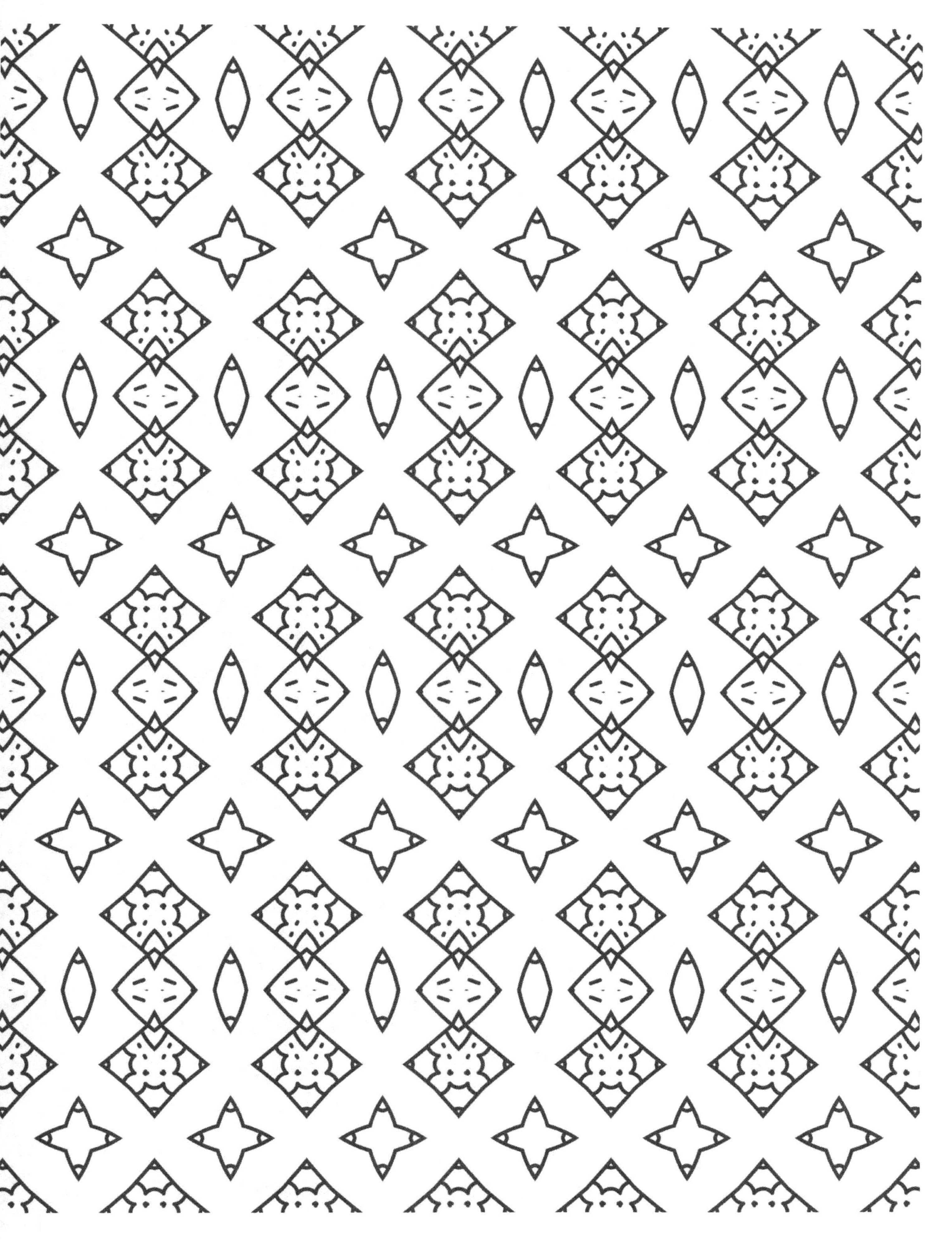

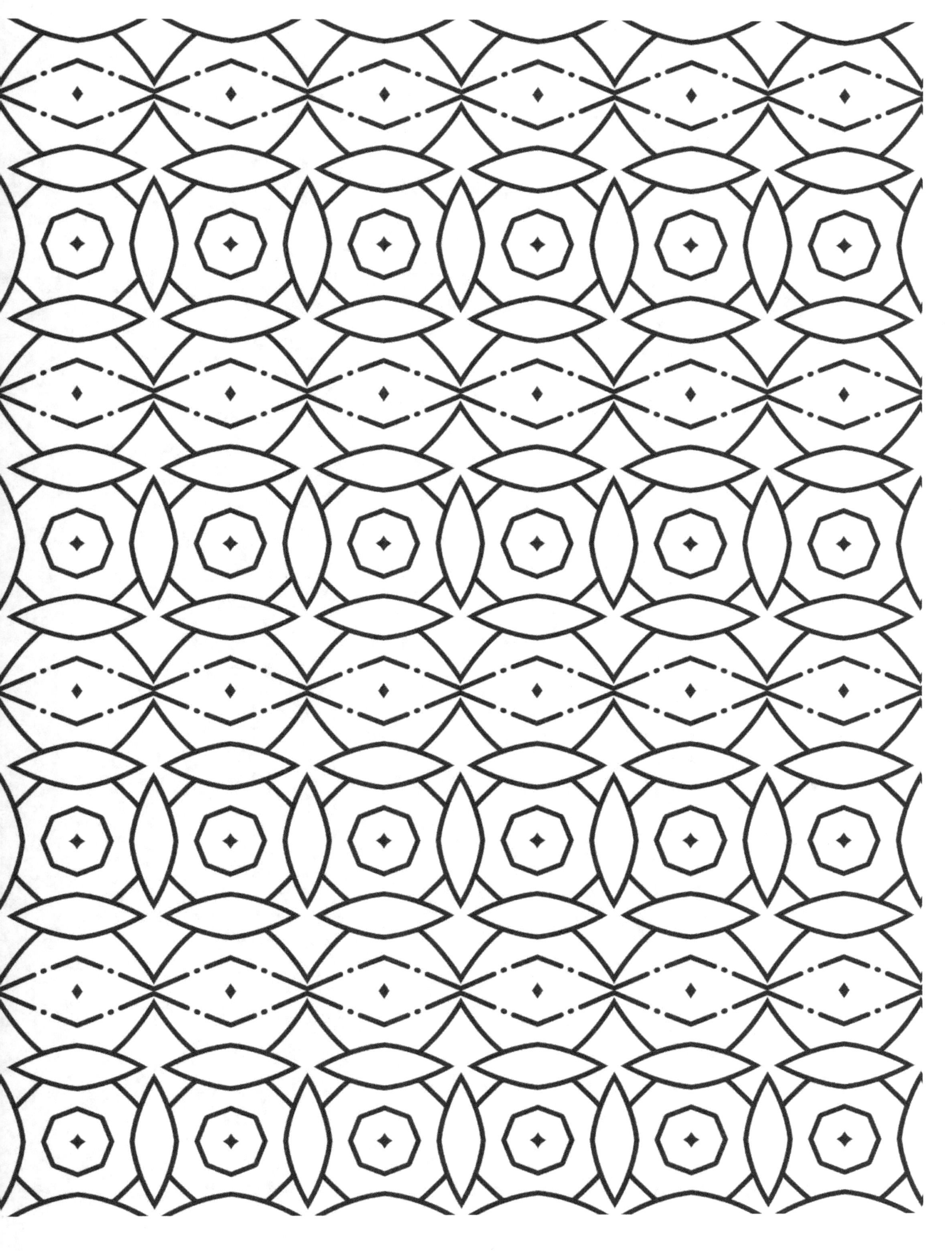

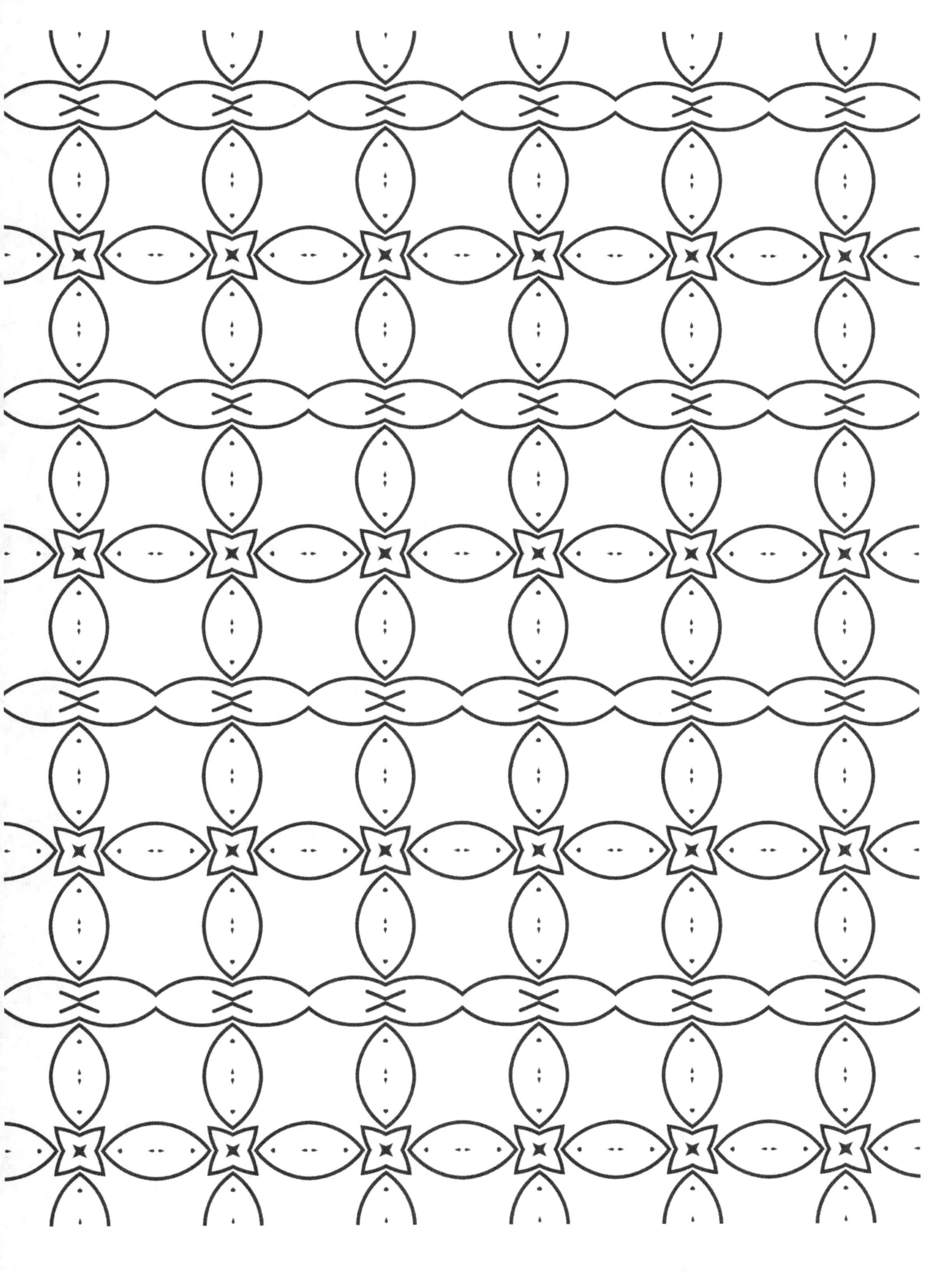

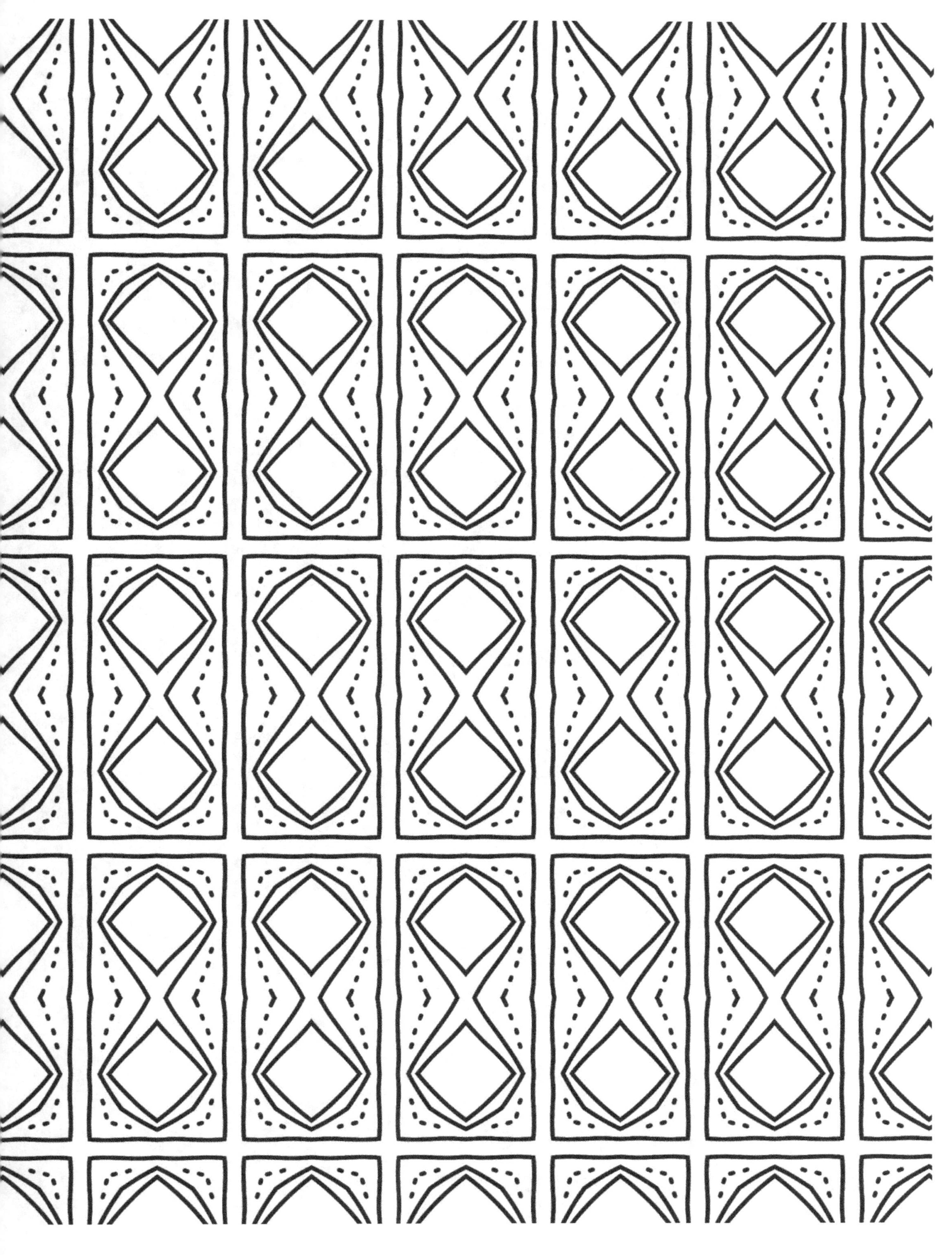

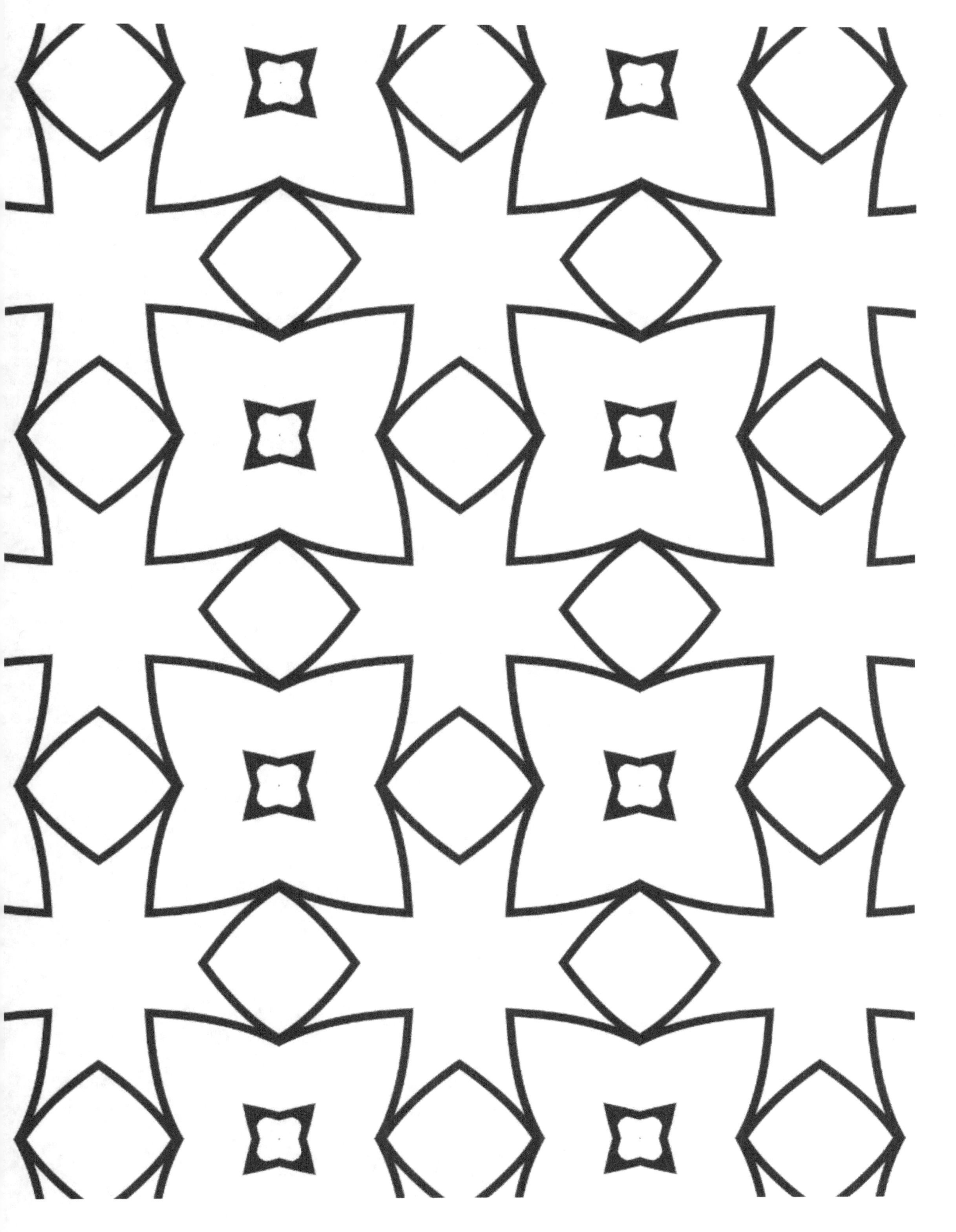

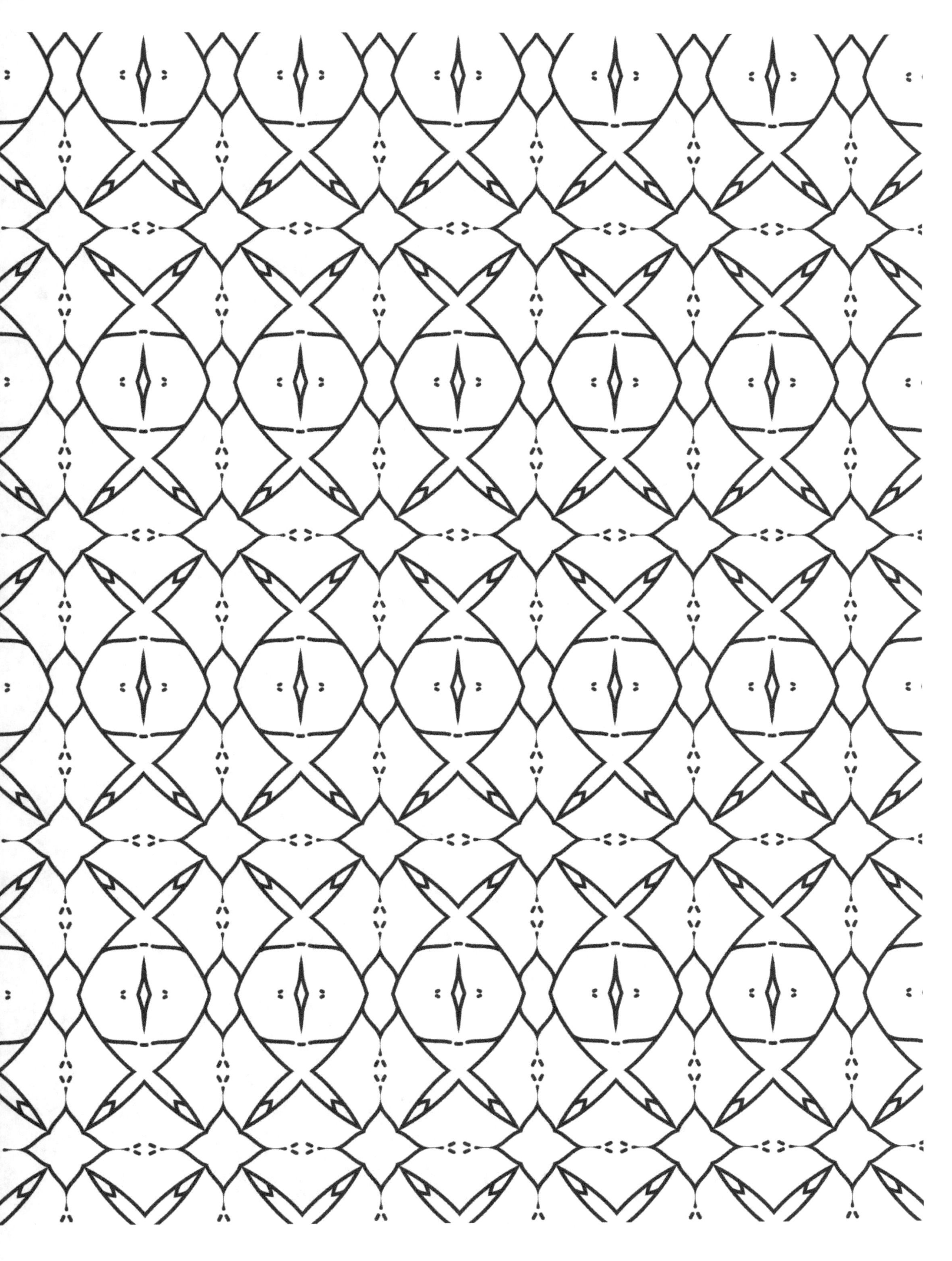

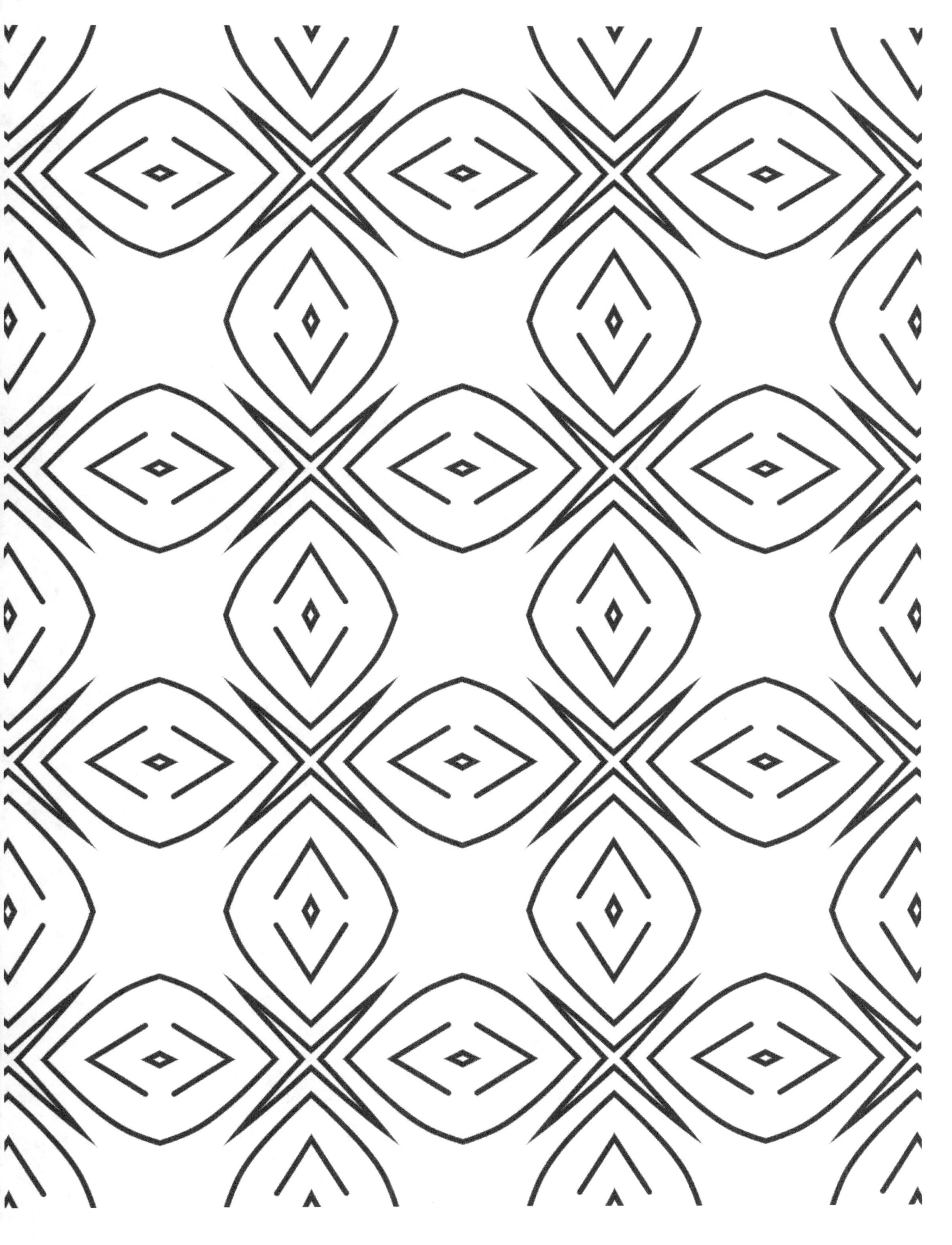

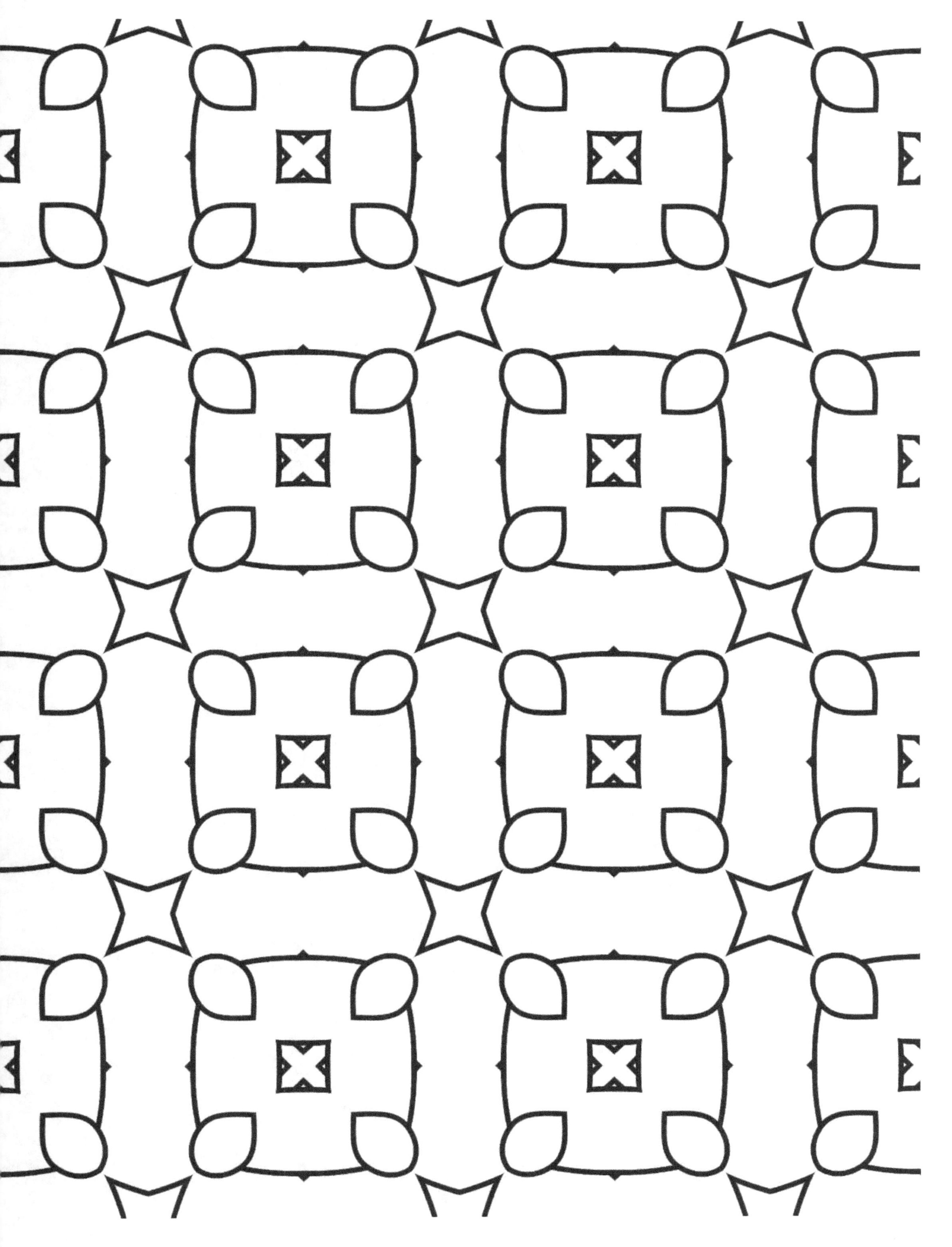

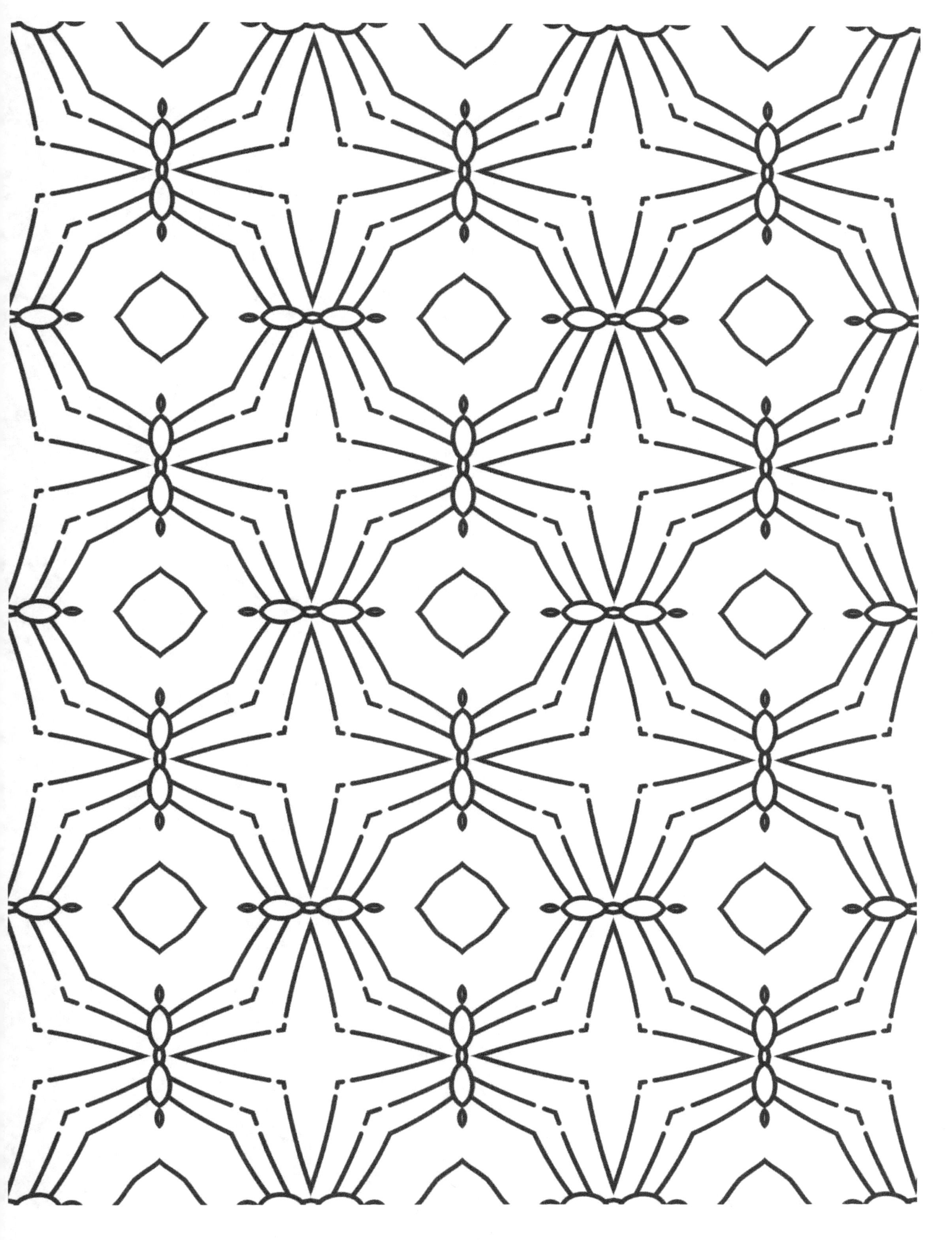